S0-AYY-661

Jeff Gordon

By Jeff Savage

AMAZING ATHLETES

LERNER**SPORTS** / **Minneapolis**

This book is available in two editions:
Library binding by LernerSports
Soft cover by First Avenue Editions
Imprints of Lerner Publishing Group
241 First Avenue North
Minneapolis, MN 55401 U.S.A.

Website address: www.lernerbooks.com

Library of Congress Cataloging-in-Publication Data

Savage, Jeff, 1961—
    Jeff Gordon / by Jeff Savage.
      p.   cm. (Amazing athletes)
    Summary: Recounts the life of race car driver Jeff Gordon, whose highly successful, record-breaking career was kicked off when he was four years old and received a quarter midget race car from his father.
    ISBN: 0-8225-1339-0 (lib. bdg. : alk. paper)
    ISBN: 0-8225-3685-4 (pbk. : alk. paper)
    1. Gordon, Jeff, 1971—Juvenile literature. 2. Automobile racing drivers—United States—Biography—Juvenile literature. [1.Gordon, Jeff, 1971—. 2. Automobile racing drivers.] I. Title.
GV1032.G67 S275 2003
796.72'092—dc21
                                                   2002009444

Manufactured in the United States of America
1 2 3 4 5 6 – DP – 08 07 06 05 04 03

TABLE OF CONTENTS

Jeff Gordon's well-known Chevy race car carries the number 24. It also has stickers on it from a lot of different companies.

A FAST RIDE

Jeff Gordon pressed his foot hard on the gas pedal. His bright-colored car—number 24— zoomed down the track at 170 miles per hour. Jeff was racing against other drivers in the 2001 Brickyard 400. The event was at the world-famous Indianapolis Motor Speedway.

Jeff has said that the key to any race is "to tell yourself be calm, be calm, be calm . . . [and] let the race unfold."

For the first forty **laps,** Jeff had been behind more than half of the other cars. By Lap 60, he was in eighteenth place. That's when he made his move. Jeff squeezed the steering wheel tightly as he swerved through traffic. He passed one car and then another. Suddenly, he was in third place and gaining fast. The crowd roared as Jeff's red, yellow, and blue car streaked by.

Helmet on, Jeff is ready to race!

After a slow start, Jeff keeps the lead for good. In 2001 he won the Brickyard 400 for the third time.

With just twenty-five laps left in the race, Jeff blew past cars driven by Sterling Marlin and Dale Jarrett to take the lead. He stayed in front the rest of the way and whizzed past the **checkered flag** for the victory. It was Jeff's third Brickyard 400 win. But as Jeff said afterward, "I don't race for statistics, I race to win. . . . Three Brickyard 400s. Whoa!"

Jeff Gordon proved again that he's the best race car driver in the world. He's not only a fierce competitor. He has nerves of steel.

Confetti pours down on Jeff. He is holding up the trophy for winning the Winston Cup Championship in 2001.

Jeff got his first taste of racing at a young age. His stepfather brought home a quarter midget car like this one.

BUILT FOR SPEED

Jeff has been racing vehicles ever since he can remember. He was born in 1971 in Vallejo, California. Jeff's father left home when Jeff was just three months old. Jeff's sister, Kim, was three years old at the time. Jeff was four in 1975, when his mother, Carol, remarried.

Jeff's new stepfather's name was John Bickford. Jeff called him Dad.

That same year, Jeff learned to ride a BMX bike. He practiced tricks on a track at the end of the street. Jeff's mother didn't think this type of biking was safe.

When Jeff's father bought him a race car, Jeff forgot all about his BMX bike. At first, Jeff's mom was shocked. Then she figured out that racing cars was actually safer then biking—even though the driver was only four years old!

Jeff's race car was a **quarter midget**. It was about six feet long and painted black. The fastest it could go was twenty miles per hour.

Jeff and his father cleared the weeds from a nearby field. Jeff practiced driving nearly every day.

By the age of five, Jeff was racing his quarter midget against older children at local California tracks. A year later, he began competing in **go-karts** that went twice as fast. At seven, he started playing video games, which helped him develop quick **reflexes**.

Jeff's quarter midget had his nickname "Gordy" painted on the hood.

Dark-haired and soft-spoken, Jeff was small for his age. By third grade, kids began teasing him. Jeff feared the bullies, but he never let them know it. A few times, he even defended himself in fights. Before long, the bullying stopped.

SATURDAY
SPORTS REVIEW

Speedy youngster becomes Quarter Midget Champion!

Jeff won his first quarter midget national championship in 1979.

SPRINTING TO THE LEAD

Jeff listened to his teachers and earned good grades in school. His reward was more racing. He and his father traveled to racetracks all over California.

In 1979, when Jeff was eight, he became the quarter midget national champion for the first time. He was competing against drivers who were twice his age. By 1981, Jeff was entering local races against teenagers. He won every race.

Sprint cars were Jeff's next challenge. He began racing them in 1983.

By the age of twelve, Jeff began practicing in a half-ton **sprint car** with a powerful 600-**horsepower** engine. But drivers had to be at least fourteen years old to compete in sprint races. Jeff tried to sneak into races by making himself look older. He drew a phony mustache on his face with an eyebrow pencil. Sometimes the trick worked, and Jeff got to race. Other times, the race officials sent him home.

Sprint racing was harder for Jeff. The other drivers were very skilled. One time, Jeff and his father traveled to Florida for a big race. Jeff's car broke down on the very first lap. Jeff cried and wished he could quit racing. But his father wouldn't let him give up.

Jeff and his father grew tired of trying to sneak into races. They learned that many racetracks in the central United States had no age limits. So in 1984, when Jeff was thirteen, his family moved to Pittsboro, Indiana. There he could compete in any race he wanted.

Outside Pittsboro is a sign that reads: "Pittsboro Welcomes you, The Hometown of Jeff Gordon, NASCAR Driver."

Within a year, Jeff won his first sprint car race. It was at K-C Raceway in Chillcothe, Ohio. When Jeff crossed the finish line, he cried tears of joy. His father ran down the hill to the center of the track. He hugged Jeff and lifted him high in the air.

In May 1990, Jeff's car edged past the car of Rich Vogler. Rich was one of Jeff's earliest rivals.

Jeff's dad *(far right)* helped Jeff celebrate winning both the sprint and midget championships in 1990.

INTO THE BIG TIME

Jeff's favorite subject in high school was science, because he learned more about how an engine works. Jeff raced most weekends and sometimes used Fridays to travel. This meant he missed school, but he always made up the work. For fun with his friends, he shot pool, skateboarded, and played video games.

Jeff poses for his graduation picture. He was about to graduate from Tri-West High School in Lizton, Indiana.

Jeff stayed in shape by running on the cross-country team of Tri-West High School. But racing was easily his favorite sport. He even competed in a race on the night of his graduation

Jeff's racing helped make him popular in high school. The other students voted him prom king during his senior year.

from Tri-West in 1989. He began competing in stock car racing soon after, when he joined the Busch Grand National circuit. He teamed with **pit crew** chief Ray Evernham.

On the Busch Grand National circuit, Jeff drove a white Ford. It carried the logo of Baby Ruth candy bars.

The Busch circuit is part of **NASCAR**, which stands for National Association for Stock Car Auto Racing. Stock cars are like regular cars that people drive on roads, except they have bigger engines. NASCAR holds races each year at tracks across the United States. Drivers collect points based on how well they race. At the end of the season, the driver with the most points wins the **points title** and the NASCAR championship.

At Hendrick Motorsports, Jeff's car had its own shop and fifteen mechanics. They wore very colorful overalls. The clothes earned them the nickname, the "Rainbow Warriors."

Jeff burst onto the NASCAR scene as a daredevil racer. In 1992, he won a record eleven **pole positions** and three victories.

A **sponsor** named Rick Hendrick was so impressed that he offered to help pay some of Jeff's expenses. In exchange, Hendrick Motorsports would get some of the **prize money**. Hendrick's company was based in Charlotte, North Carolina. Jeff and his parents moved there later in 1992.

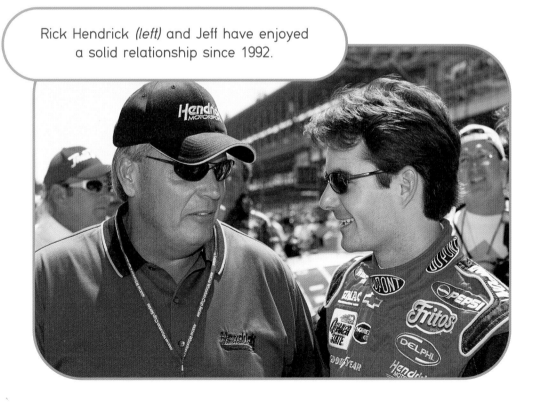

Rick Hendrick *(left)* and Jeff have enjoyed a solid relationship since 1992.

The next step up from the Busch circuit was the Winston Cup circuit. Jeff became the Winston Cup Rookie of the Year in 1993.

In 1993, Jeff became a rookie on the Winston Cup circuit—the top level of NASCAR. The day before the Daytona 500 in Florida, Jeff competed in the 125-mile **qualifying race** against the best stock car racers in the world. Jeff shocked everyone by winning the race. Afterward, he met Miss Winston, Brooke Sealey. Jeff and Brooke soon began dating. A year later, they were married.

Brooke Sealey was a student at the University of North Carolina when she met Jeff in 1993.

Throughout the 1990s, Jeff raced against NASCAR's best drivers. These included Dale Earnhardt, who drove his famous number 3 Chevy.

WINNING THE RACE

Jeff won his first points race in the middle of the 1994 NASCAR season at the Coca-Cola 600 in Charlotte. Afterward, Jeff told reporters: "This is the greatest moment of my life, a feeling I will never forget." Six weeks later, Jeff won his second race. The next day, he read in the newspaper that he'd been given a nickname, "The Kid."

Jeff holds up a trophy for winning
his first Brickyard 400 in 1994.

Jeff signs autographs for a few of his millions of fans.

Jeff roared out front in 1995 and never looked back. He cruised to his first Winston Cup points title to become the youngest champion of the modern era. Jeff was a famous celebrity. Companies created Jeff Gordon souvenir T-shirts, caps, sunglasses, key chains, coffee mugs, and yo-yos.

Jeff enjoyed his popularity, but he ignored all the fuss and concentrated on winning. He won ten races in 1996 to earn $3.5 million in prize money. Then he won ten more races in 1997 and claimed his second points title. Jeff was determined to become even better. But how could he possibly top two ten-win seasons in a row? By winning thirteen times!

In 1997, Jeff celebrated winning his second Winston Cup points title.

Jeff tied the modern record in 1998 for most wins in a season. "I have to admit," Jeff said, "that at my age, you're not expected to do all this. It's amazing to me I've gotten this far."

In the early 2000s, Jeff faced some challenges. He and pit crew chief Ray Evernham parted ways. Throughout the 2000 racing season, Jeff struggled without Ray. He won three times and placed ninth in the points standings. Jeff and his new pit crew chief, Robbie Loomis, worked hard to improve Jeff's car.

Jeff has come to rely on the skills of his pit crew chief, Robbie Loomis.

The speed of the Rainbow Warriors in the pit helped Jeff capture his third Brickyard 400 victory in 2001.

The hard work paid off in 2001, when Jeff roared to his fourth Winston Cup points title. His favorite victory was his third win at the Brickyard 400, the day after his thirtieth birthday. The next year, though, Brooke and Jeff separated, and Brooke filed for divorce.

A young fan asks Jeff a question at a
Kids and the Hood event.

Jeff has become motorsports' all-time
money winner. He is rich beyond his wildest
dreams. He owns a mansion, a speedboat, and
a Lear jet. Jeff also gives a lot of his money
away. He donates to the Make-A-Wish
Foundation and to cancer research. He created
an organization called Kids and the Hood that
helps children.

Jeff's message to kids is simple: "Don't Ever
Quit." When it comes to racing, fans know that
Jeff Gordon won't ever quit.

Selected Career Highlights

2002 Won his sixtieth race, youngest driver ever to do so

2001 Won fourth Winston Cup points title, only third driver to do so
Became first NASCAR driver to win more than $10 million in one year

2000 Became the youngest Winston Cup driver in history to win fifty races
Won at Sears Point Raceway a record sixth straight year

1999 Won seven Winston Cup races
Was first-ever driver to win the most races five years in a row

1998 Won Winston Cup points title
Won a record-tying thirteen Winston Cup races

1997 Won Winston Cup points title
Became the youngest driver ever to win the Daytona 500

1996 Finished second overall in Winston Cup points

1995 Won his first Winston Cup points title, youngest driver to do so

1994 Won his first Brickyard 400 race at Indianapolis Motor Speedway

1993 Named Winston Cup Rookie of the Year

1992 Moved up from Busch Grand National to Winston Cup circuit

1991 Won National Dirt Track Championship

1990 Won USAC Midget Championship
Won USAC Sprint Championship

GLOSSARY

checkered flag: the black-and-white flag that is waved at the end of a race

go-kart: a small, flat, one-person vehicle with a motor that is used for racing (called karting)

horsepower: a measure of an engine's power; the greater the horsepower, the faster the car

lap: one complete go-around on a racetrack. A NASCAR race typically is made up of hundreds of laps.

NASCAR: the National Association for Stock Car Auto Racing. Founded in 1947, NASCAR is the governing group of stock-car racing. It says which changes to a car's engine and body allow it to keep its "stock car" status.

pit crew: a team of mechanics that works on a car during a pit stop. A pit stop happens when the driver pulls off the racetrack and his or her car is adjusted and refueled.

points title: an award given each year to the NASCAR driver who has earned the most points throughout the racing season

pole position: the inside front row—the best position—at the start of a race. The driver who gets this position was the fastest in the qualifying race held before the real race.

prize money: the money awarded to each driver based on the driver's finish in a race

qualifying race: a race that takes place before the real race to determine the starting order of all the cars. The fastest car in the qualifying race wins the pole position for the real race.

quarter midget: a race car that is larger than a go-kart but smaller than a sprint car

reflex: an automatic response, done without thinking

sponsor: someone who pays for a driver's car, pit crew, travel, and other expenses in return for a share of the driver's prize winnings. The driver also pastes the sponsor's logo all over the race car as a form of advertising.

sprint car: a race car that is larger than a quarter midget but smaller than a stock car. It has a powerful engine.

FURTHER READING & WEBSITES

Christopher, Matt. *On the Track with Jeff Gordon*. New York: Little Brown & Company, 2001.

Kirkpatrick, Rob. *Jeff Gordon: Nascar Champion*. New York: Powerkids Press, 2000.

Johnstone, Mike. *NASCAR*. Minneapolis, MN: LernerSports, 2002.

Savage, Jeff. *Jeff Gordon: Racing's Superstar*. Minneapolis, MN: LernerSports, 2000.

Sherman, Josepha. *Jeff Gordon*. Crystal Lake, IL: Heinemann Library, 2001.

Stewart, Mark. *Jeff Gordon: Rainbow Warrior*. Brookfield, CT: The Millbrook Press, 2000.

Jeff Gordon Online
<http://www.gordonline.com>
A fan website that gives loads of information not only about Jeff but also about the Hendrick Motorsports team and general NASCAR information and links.

NASCAR Website
<http://www.nascar.com>
A website developed by NASCAR that provides fans with recent news stories, biographies of drivers, and information about racing teams and race cars.

The Official Website
<http://www.jeffgordon.com>
Jeff's official website, featuring games, trivia, photos, and information about auto racing.

Sports Illustrated for Kids
<http://www.sikids.com>
The *Sports Illustrated for Kids* website that covers all sports, including auto racing.

INDEX

PHOTO ACKNOWLEDGMENTS

Photos reproduced with the permission of: © ALLSPORT USA/Craig Jones, pp. 4, 29; © SportsChrome East/West, pp. 5, 25; © Scott McNair, M.D., pp. 6, 7, 19, 26, 27; © Stephanie Maze/CORBIS, p. 8; Bill Hauser, p. 11; © John Mahoney, pp. 12, 14, 15; © Seth Poppel Yearbook Archives, p. 16; © SportsChrome East/West/Greg Crisp, pp. 17, 20, 21, 24; © ALLSPORT USA/Robert LaBerge, p. 22; © James Cutler, p. 23; © Tom Raymond, courtesy DuPont Company, p. 28.

Cover: © ALLSPORT USA/David Taylor (top); © Scott McNair, M.D. (bottom)